Ana Paula dos Santos Barreto
Ana Carolina Feitosa

A Haemodialysis Case:

Ana Paula dos Santos Barreto
Ana Carolina Feitosa

A Haemodialysis Case:

The Importance of Psychological Care in the Hospital Setting

ScienciaScripts

Imprint
Any brand names and product names mentioned in this book are subject to trademark, brand or patent protection and are trademarks or registered trademarks of their respective holders. The use of brand names, product names, common names, trade names, product descriptions etc. even without a particular marking in this work is in no way to be construed to mean that such names may be regarded as unrestricted in respect of trademark and brand protection legislation and could thus be used by anyone.

Cover image: www.ingimage.com

This book is a translation from the original published under ISBN 978-3-330-99992-3.

Publisher:
Sciencia Scripts
is a trademark of
Dodo Books Indian Ocean Ltd. and OmniScriptum S.R.L publishing group

120 High Road, East Finchley, London, N2 9ED, United Kingdom
Str. Armeneasca 28/1, office 1, Chisinau MD-2012, Republic of Moldova, Europe
Printed at: see last page
ISBN: 978-620-8-21515-6

One day, when you look back, you'll see that the most beautiful days were the ones you fought for.

Sigmund Freud

SUMMARY

1 INTRODUCTION

Hospital psychology is a relatively new area of psychology, but it is a field that has expanded significantly. Its work takes place in various sectors of the hospital, not only in the wards, dealing with the patient in bed, but also in the outpatient clinic and some specific sectors, depending on the hospital. They work with the psychic aspects of physical illness, the patient's relationship with their illness and the hospitalization process.

Thus, Hospital Psychology and Hospitals are relevant aspects to be addressed, due to their recent emergence. In view of this, the corresponding peculiarities will be discussed, with regard to the role and importance of the psychologist in the general hospital, since it is well known that the hospitalized patient suffers not only physically, but also psychically, precisely because of this hospitalization, which leads to an abrupt change in a life that was, in many cases, active and independent, causing not only a loss of autonomy but also of privacy.

So what is the importance of psychological care in the hospital setting? This importance is evidenced by the fact that it contributes greatly to patients being able to deal with their illness, working on the relationship that the patient has with his symptom, showing the important role of the psychologist in the hospital setting, a place that differs from others due to its peculiarities, however, even in the face of difficulties encountered, it is possible to carry out psychological care in this space, regardless of the necessary interruptions, using listening as a working tool clinical approach based on the patient's speech, with the aim of allowing them to elaborate on the issues that affect their subjectivity.

Even in the case of a chronic illness, which needs to be treated permanently, psychological care helps patients to get through each stage in the least painful way possible, because what can't be cured seeks quality of life. This importance is corroborated when doctors realize that the patient's treatment goes beyond medication, which is when the hospital psychologist is asked to provide psychological care.

Because treatment is something that causes both physical and psychological suffering to the patient, it is essential to investigate in more detail the patient's relationship with their illness, because subjectivity is affected and each patient is peculiar in the way they deal with what happens to them.

This fact is particularly pertinent to why this topic was chosen, because even though the patient understands that it is necessary to undergo invasive treatment and procedures, they cause anguish, fear and anxiety in relation to waiting for news of the prognosis of their clinical condition, which sometimes leads to resistance to the hospital routine, making the work of the medical team and their relationship with it difficult.

As a result, even though hospital psychology is expanding, it is often noticed that the hospital psychologist is asked by the medical team to be an integrator of the multidisciplinary team and to contribute, from his knowledge, uniting it with the other knowledge, making a total contribution to the patient's recovery.

Therefore, the aim of this study is to examine, through a case study, the clinical crossings equivalent to the subjectivity of a patient undergoing hemodialysis treatment in a general hospital.

The data collected refers to the subjective aspects inherent in the patient's relationship with their chronic illness, the procedure being based on the consultations carried out with the patient and the discussions resulting from the interconsultations.

Thus, in view of the patient's subjective way of dealing with their illness and going through each hemodialysis session, some concepts from psychoanalysis will be linked to the subject of this paper.

As this is a qualitative study, data analysis was based on listening to the patient, interconsultations with the health team and information gathered from his medical records.

Therefore, the scope of this work is the study of the crossings in a patient undergoing hemodialysis treatment, based on the construction of a case study, using clinical listening through the psychoanalytic approach as the method for analyzing the content of the data collected.

However, there are still ambiguous concepts regarding the role of psychology in general hospitals. Therefore, in terms of academic and social relevance, this work aims to discuss issues to elucidate the importance of psychology's work in this context so that it can be understood, showing its effectiveness and relevant contribution, thus demystifying misconceptions about this area so that there is a better understanding by the health team of the benefits of this work in the general hospital and consequently better overall patient care.

Thus, this paper presents the psychoanalytic approach as a guide to the care provided, discussing its obstacles and also its possibilities, supported by authors such as Simonetti, Freud and Moretto, showing its techniques brought from the clinic, but adapted to a new context in which to practice, because from the clinical perspective as an expansion in a space created by the psychologist in the hospital, it is also necessary to clarify the peculiarities of the setting, which differs from the traditional consulting room.

In addition, the clinical case presented corroborates the theory explained, illustrating and enriching this work, showing in practice what is found in the theory studied.

Today, the importance of hospital psychologists is a reality and their work with patients who are hospitalized or undergoing treatment makes them a key player in caring for their patients' psychiatric health.

2 PSYCHOLOGY AND ITS ENTRY INTO THE HOSPITAL

Health professionals today have realized the importance of integrality in patient treatment, as it is a biopsychosocial issue behind the disease or organ being treated. This is due to the results obtained by bringing psychologists into the hospital to care for the sick person and not to treat their illness, as medicine already treats this.

Thus, albeit timidly, psychology has been achieving its place in the hospital and over time, the presence of a psychologist as part of the healthcare team in the hospital institution has become increasingly indispensable.

Therefore, it is important to discuss pertinent issues since the entry of psychology into the general hospital and the paths it has traveled over time, showing its important and indispensable role in this space.

2.1 PSYCHOLOGY AND ITS ROLE IN HOSPITAL INSTITUTIONS

The hospital is often referred to as a place for the sick and also for healing. It is also a place where treatment can be long or short, depending on the pathology of each patient. Therefore, when people talk about hospitals, the general idea is that their health has been damaged in some way, causing them to go through the process of hospitalization. This is a process feared by the patient and also by their family members, who are not always aware of the illness, and consequently do not know how to deal with this new situation.

Thus, for the World Health Organization apud Campos (1995, p.20):

> The hospital is an integral part of a coordinated health system, whose function is to provide the community with complete preventive and

> curative medical care, including services extended to the family at home, and also a training center for those working in the field of health and for biosocial research.

It is therefore understood that medical care goes beyond patient care alone, extending to the family as well, as they also deserve subsidies for maintaining their health, as well as preventing illnesses, while also providing the community with curative care and various treatments. It is also concerned with investing in research in order to better train those who work in the field of health, with the aim of strengthening and improving individual and collective care in society.

The care or treatment of hospitalized patients provides the family with greater knowledge about the disease in question and also the care that their sick family member needs, as well as the prevention of other family members so that there is less chance of this and other illnesses occurring.

In this way, the Ministry of Health apud Campos (ibid, p.20), defined the concept of hospital:

> The hospital is an integral part of a medical and social organization, whose basic function is to provide the population with complete medical and health care, both curative and preventive, under any system of care, including home care, and whose external services radiate into the family environment. It is also a center for education, training of human resources and health research, as well as patient referrals, and is responsible for supervising and guiding the health establishments technically linked to it. The hospital is also a center for medical and health training and biosocial research.

From the aforementioned definitions of the hospital, it is clear what its functions are in terms of what it provides and enables for the population in terms of health care, as well as its reach beyond its doors, which has become a place not only for healing but also for disease prevention, together with health education and research, including biological and social investigation of the community.

Campos (1995) also states that the hospital is a biopsychosocial research center and should therefore be understood as a whole, with the aim of maintaining man's physical, social and mental well-being.

Therefore, as defined by the World Health Organization (WHO) apud Oliveira and Angelucci (2012, p.158), health is understood as a "state of complete physical, mental and social well-being, and not just the absence of illness or disease", where it is firstly highlighted that the understanding of being human is understood here, by several dimensions, admitting that not only individual but also social aspects can affect health, highlighting various ways of living and relating. Also significant is the commitment to quality of life, which does not mean not being ill, but rather the conditions to expand one's potential.

Article 196 of the Federal Constitution (1988) defines it this way:

> Health is the right of all and the duty of the state, guaranteed through social and economic policies aimed at reducing the risk of disease and other illnesses and universal and equal access to support and services for their promotion, protection and recovery.

Thus, based on this principle, Salto's (2007) statement about the emergence of Hospital Psychology is relevant in 1818, when McLean Hospital was founded in Massachusetts, where the first multi-professional team was formed, including psychologists. In the same hospital, in 1904, a psychology laboratory was founded, made up of pathologists, physiologists, biochemists and psychologists, where pioneering research into hospital psychology was carried out.

The assumptions behind the emergence of hospital psychology are the influence of psychic aspects on organic diseases, resolutive care for discharged patients, adherence to treatment facilitated by emotional aspects and the humanization of working conditions and patient care. However, this is a relatively new area, where the presence and work of psychologists in hospitals has become increasingly frequent over time, as hospital health teams have noticed that there is something beyond the physical symptom that needs to be treated and that medicine doesn't always meet this demand. As a result, hospital psychologists have been asked to deal with these issues. Thus, albeit slowly, this activity has been gaining strength and showing its value and importance over time.

Kern and BornHoldt (2002) state that Hospital Psychology is an exclusively Brazilian term and does not exist in other countries, since abroad this area is called Health Psychology, thus leaving a certain lack of equivalence between the terms hospital and health.

The importance of this exclusive term is highlighted by Campos (1995), when he states that the history of hospital psychology in Brazil can be traced back to 1954 in Sao Paulo, when the work of Dr. Mathilde Neder, a pioneer, began her work in hospital psychology at the Hospital das Clínicas, preparing children for spinal surgery, at the then Clinica de Ortopedia e Traumatologia, now the Institute of Orthopedics and Traumatology.

Therefore, it is worth noting that according to Gioia-Martins (2012, p.25), psychologists began to work in integrated health agencies (AIS) from 1983, with the first Brazilian psychologists working in health services in public hospitals.

Hospital psychology is now a specialty in Brazilian psychology and although this path has not been so easy in our country, according to Ismael (2010), in 1997 the Brazilian Society of Hospital Psychology (SBPH) was founded by 45 psychologists who worked in hospitals in various Brazilian states and which seeks to encourage research in the area and increasingly organize the profession. The SBPH has therefore been strengthening this area of psychology, further promoting the professionals who work in this field and aiming to broaden the field of scientific knowledge.

Thus, Simonetti (2013, p.21) states that:

> When medical discourse fails in its epistemological claim to banish subjectivity, the doors of the hospital are then opened for psychology to enter, enter and take care of those things that subvert the medical order, that create confusion and perplexity on the hospital scene.

This author's perspective can be complemented by that of Romano (1999), who argues that when doctors and health professionals realized that there is something beyond physical illness, that it is an unconscious issue that causes complaints and conflicts, complicating clinical progress and reducing therapeutic effectiveness, the importance of the psychologist's presence in the hospital was recognized. They found that emotional aspects can interfere with adherence to treatment in a way that modifies it and enables decisions to be made that influence the chances of survival.

The hospitalized patient is out of their daily life, out of their flow, out of their family life and out of work. They go to the hospital for organic reasons, to cure their illness, to treat something physical that makes them feel unwell, which requires hospitalization or treatment, which directly interferes with the patient's emotional aspects. It is therefore around the anguish, fears, etc., caused by this hospitalization that psychology is present, with the aim of contributing to the total well-being of this patient.

Thus, Botega (2012, p.43) states that:

> When our body is silent, we often forget about it. This body that seems so "ours", something so taken for granted, that has been given to us, that normally submits to our desires and obeys our orders. In the depths of our mind, our body is immortal. As for illness, it serves to remind us that we have a body, that we can die. The feeling of a person who suddenly finds themselves seriously ill is that they are no longer their own master. The experience is of becoming a slave to the body and to time. How a person reacts to this situation depends on many factors: their personality, their history, their beliefs, their emotional state, the support they can receive and accept, and time.

Faced with the illness and, consequently, the

hospitalization, the patient is faced with limitations and loses his

In addition, the patient's identity is also lost: during hospitalization, the patient is now identified as just one part of the body, i.e. the illness itself and/or the bed number. All these changes cause suffering for the patient, who is now prevented from carrying out their normal activities. This afflicts the patient to such an extent that they become disinterested in anything that has nothing to do with their health condition. The patient is then reduced to his illness, his suffering, and is not interested in anything that has nothing to do with what makes him suffer, i.e. his illness in question.

Therefore, according to Freud ([1914] 2006, p.89):

> [...] It is common knowledge, and I accept it as normal, that a person tormented by pain and organic malaise ceases to be interested in the things of the external world, insofar as they do not concern his suffering. A closer look also teaches us that he also withdraws libidinal interest from his love objects: while suffering, he stops loving [...] We should then say: the sick man withdraws his libidinal cathexis back into his own ego and puts it out again when he recovers.

Hospitalized patients are unable to go about their daily lives, turning all their attention and anxiety to their illness. This can have a detrimental effect on the patient's recovery, even leading to prolonged hospitalization.

In view of this, Dias and Radomile (2006) state that the plausible reason for setting up a psychology service in a general hospital is that the psychological treatment of patients admitted to these hospitals can bring important therapeutic benefits and advantages, such as better adherence to medical treatment, faster recovery and, consequently, shorter hospital stays, less use of medical services and, therefore, a reduction in healthcare costs, among others.

The concept of hospital psychology is based on the understanding of various authors who discuss this area of psychology, in terms of what it is about, as well as its work and actions aimed at promoting the total health of hospitalized patients.

Therefore, according to Lazzaretti (2007), it is understood that

Hospital Psychology as an offshoot of Clinical Psychology in hospital institutions. The approach to subjectivity, a characteristic This statement makes it clear that, regardless of where the subject is, it is possible to approach them and develop therapeutic work from there. This statement makes it clear that regardless of where the subject is, it is possible to approach them and develop a therapeutic work from then on, because what is wanted is to treat what is not palpable and for this, as long as the subject is willing to talk about their anguish, psychological care takes place.

2.2 HOSPITAL PSYCHOLOGY AND ITS PURPOSES

The aim of hospital psychology is to understand and treat the way in which each patient deals with their illness and the process of hospitalization and/or treatment, because during this process, the subjectivity of this individual is affected and therefore needs to be heard.

Thus, for Simonetti (2013, p.15) "Hospital psychology and the

field of understanding and treating the psychological aspects of illness". Hospital psychology deals not only with illnesses with psychic causes, classified as "psychosomatic", but also with any and all illnesses, as these have, without exception, psychological aspects full of subjectivity, This is the objective to be achieved by triggering a process of symbolic elaboration of the illness as a way of helping the patient to get through their experience of being ill, because medicine already deals with the real record, in other words, while medicine excludes the patient's subjectivity, psychology immerses itself in this same subjectivity.

Thus, working through words is valid, even if the patient is unable to speak for various reasons, because there are many non-verbal signs with the value of words and what matters to psychology is the relationship that the patient has with their symptom and not the illness itself. Hospital psychology achieves its strategy of working with illness in the symbolic register by using two techniques: analytical listening, which brings together free association, interpretation, transference analysis, etc.; situational management, with interventions aimed at the concrete situation formed around the illness.

Simonetti (Ibid., p.16) also states that:

> Hospital psychology emphasizes the psychic part, but it doesn't say that the other part isn't important. On the contrary, it will always ask what the psychic reaction is to this organic reality, what the subject's position is in the face of this "real" illness, and it will make this its working material.

In this way, it is understood that the work of hospital psychology revolves around the subject's psychic response to their organic illness, which is real and needs to be treated as much as their psychological aspect in relation to this reality during the hospitalization process, working on the subject's positioning in relation to their illness.

Therefore, Camon (1994, p.23) states that "the main objective of hospital psychology is to minimize the suffering caused by hospitalization". In this way, there is also a need to cover the sequelae and emotional consequences of hospitalization, as well as minimizing the suffering caused by it. Thus, in order for care to be successful, the variables of this field of action must be considered, where the fact of being hospitalized must be understood as a consequence of this process and its implications for the patient's life, not just reduced to the process of institutionalization.

The aim of the psychologist, according to Sebastiani (2003), is to highlight the importance of their work since many pathologies are aggravated by the emotional aspects of the patient, where the psychologist's role will be essential for the recovery/improvement of the patient's general health.

Some of the places where the psychologist can work in the hospital are the outpatient clinic, where the patient may be referred by the doctor or because they are excessively worried about their health; in the inpatient units or wards, where the patient cannot go home because of their illness and loses their individuality, feeling attacked by the hospital routine and its rigid schedule, which can lead to a process of depersonalization; another place of care is the Intensive Care Unit (ICU), which requires more intensive, fast and efficient care from the team, where the family cannot often stay and the psychologist in this case becomes a link between patient/team/family. It is important to note that each hospital has different specialties as a reference for treatment, as there are hospitals, for example, that do not have an emergency unit, so not all of them have the same treatment and care sectors.

Therefore, according to Camon (2003), psychologists need to be clearly aware that their work is not just restricted to psychotherapy, but also to dealing with the possible emotional sequelae caused by the internment. This process of

Hospitalization needs to be viewed broadly, as a set of factors that are a consequence of this process and also its implications for the patient's life, since hospital psychologists often don't have their own place to work. Often, this is done on the wards and ends up being interrupted by hospital staff involved in their basic work (nurses, cleaning staff, etc.). In this case, all these factors will have to be taken into account by the psychologist. Remembering that the patient will be approached in their own bed, unlike those who seek psychological care of their own volition, makes the limitations of this professional very clear, as it is important that they act without becoming an additional intrusion and a critical point in the hospitalization process.

It is therefore clearer how important this professional is, not only as the one who treats the patient directly, but also as an integrator of the patient with the family and the hospital doctors, as Simonetti (2013, p. 18) states:

> As well as considering these people individually, hospital psychology also deals with the relationships between them, constituting a true liaison psychology, with the function of facilitating relationships between patients, family members and doctors.

The psychologist's work is wide-ranging, assisting patients, their families and healthcare teams, and he or she must be aware of his or her limitations. They develop their own style of communication with patients and their families. The request for psychological care can be formal, with a request for an opinion (in the medical record) or informal: over the phone, in the corridor, on the wards, etc., the return is by medical record/bulletin or opinion sheet/interconsultation. When assisting family members, the psychologist provides information, facilitating the team-patient and family-team relationship. If there is a crisis and family maladjustment, they work on feelings of guilt, anxiety, defensive attitudes, aggression, etc.

For Ismael (2010), the psychologist's work is not done individually. Therefore, there is no doubt that teamwork is of the utmost importance, where each professional looks at the patient in a specific way, but unites their knowledge so that there is a comprehensive view, aiming to reassure both the patient and their family, with the aim of caring for this patient as a total being. The multi-professional team needs to interact in order to benefit the patient, carrying out this work in an interdisciplinary way with an exchange of information, the same language and information passed on to the patient, this attitude must be collaborative and complementary with the ability to listen to the other. Even if we come to the conclusion that each professional has his or her own specificity, this does not invalidate the other's knowledge. Help for the patient comes precisely from the exchange between the various specialties and greater understanding of the patient. However, contact between doctor and patient is not always friendly.

Thus, Botega (2012, p.50) states that:

> The relationship between doctor and patient will be an exercise in patience and perseverance, in which one will come to know a lot about the other. In the case of some conditions, particularly functional disorders, and patients with certain personality traits, the doctor-patient relationship will be shaken at various points during treatment. The patient may become demanding, hostile and uncooperative. Some patients will have already been to several professionals, including the most prestigious ones, and the feeling they transmit to the new doctor is that he will be just one more in a list of failures. In these cases, it is essential to carefully evaluate the relationship established between the patient and their previous doctors. Identify and try to understand the feelings that this patient arouses: frustration, anger, boredom.

The importance of this professional, according to Simonetti (2013), is also due to the fact that he is not only the one who treats the patient directly, but also the one who integrates the patient with the family and the hospital doctors. Since the sudden disruption of daily life in the face of hospitalization is the first difficulty experienced by the family in the face of a loved one suffering from a disease, it generates anxiety, exacerbating feelings of uncertainty, fear, loss of privacy and individuality in a strange environment.

With regard to how the psychologist can approach the patient in their bed, Ismael (2010) states that the psychological interview is essential, as it is a fundamental tool where research is the main objective, as well as providing some relief from anxiety and can be a way for the patient to express their problem. The focal interview is where we try to understand the patient, considering the moment they are going through, their illness and consequently their hospitalization.

According to Romano (1999), it is neither the place nor the obstacles that enable and shape the work. The effectiveness of the action results from a timely and pertinent therapeutic aspect, as well as clear objectives to be achieved, enabling efficient exchanges with the team, the consensus that psychological intervention with patients and their families positively interferes in the process of becoming ill and hospitalization.

Corroborating this, Penna (1992) apud Simonetti (2013, p. 157) states that: "It is true that the hospital environment is adverse to psychotherapeutic activity, but it does not prevent it, provided, of course, that the psychologist finds a flexible and creative posture aimed at circumventing the difficulties."

Given this, the work of the hospital psychologist is, after all, with the symbolic body that is in the words, as Simonetti (Ibid) states, because it is through these that the psychological aspect of illness is fundamentally worked on. Even when the patient is unable to speak, due to some medical procedure or resistance, it is still valid to guide the work through speech, which in some cases can be through gestures, because those who don't speak are spoken to, and the dialogue between psychologist and patient is the gateway to a world of meanings and senses.

Simonetti (2013) also states that hospital psychologists have a wide field of activity and can work in public clinical and psychiatric hospitals, as well as in private hospitals. They can also work in municipal and state health clinics and clinics, mental health programs, NGOs and private medical specialty clinics.

Psychology is thus progressively gaining a foothold in hospitals and is developing, improving existing services and seeking new methods of care in this area, always aiming to contribute to a better process of hospitalization and/or treatment for patients.

In view of this, it is well known that each hospital has its own specific characteristics, with different types of care, and in each specific sector there is a different working dynamic for the health team.

Therefore, this work, alluding to the clinical practice of the professional internship in hospital psychology, discusses the hemodialysis sector. This is a place where patients whose kidneys are paralyzed undergo a procedure using a machine (dialyzer), which is an artificial kidney that cleans and filters the blood with the main function of removing toxins and excess water from the body. In addition, this treatment enables the proper functioning of other organs and also aims to control blood pressure and help the body maintain a balance of substances such as sodium, potassium, urea and creatinine, including having to check your weight before and after each session to see how much fluid you have lost during the treatment.

The most common causes for a patient to have their kidneys paralyzed and consequently undergo hemodialysis treatment are hypertension and diabetes, which are systemic diseases that can occur in any age group.

This internship took place at the Gafree and Guinle University Hospital (HUGG), located in the city of Rio de Janeiro, where the hemodialysis sector is a physically small environment, made up of a team of one doctor and three or four nurses every day, with seven dialysis machines.

Therefore, it is important to highlight the problem of the hemodialysis therapeutic setting, which is not one of the most favorable, and does not provide privacy for psychological care, since it is an environment open to the circulation of the health team, for recurrent interventions with the patient.

However, this does not compromise the care itself, since its effectiveness does not depend on a completely peaceful environment for it to take place. This is therefore one of the challenges faced by psychologists in hospitals during their clinical practice.

2.3 ABOUT CHRONIC ILLNESS

Chronic diseases are those that are considered incurable in the light of medicine, but which can be treated, in many cases very effectively, i.e. there is no cure, but there are treatments so that the patient can live a better life and, above all, a better quality of life. Therefore, the permanence of this pathology necessarily changes the patient's life and, to a certain extent, that of his family, because undergoing treatment requires a reorganization of daily life, and the subjectivity of this subject is consequently affected.

Indeed, Botega (2012) states that the limitations imposed by certain chronic illnesses are not always accepted by patients and their families. At the onset of chronicity, many relatives consider the patient to be an innocent victim. However, later they may see them as a burden and a nuisance.

Therefore, Zozaya apud Santos and Sebastiani (2013, p. 149), defines chronic illness as:

> Any pathological condition that has one or more of the following characteristics: that is permanent, that leaves residual disability, which produces non-reversible pathological changes, which requires rehabilitation or which requires long periods of observation, control and care.

Unlike an acute state, chronic illness is not just a moment to be lived through; on the contrary, it is a state in which the illness remains, requiring the patient to learn to live with it. Therefore, the irreversibility of the illness is something that has a major impact on the patient's life in many ways.

Therefore, according to Santos and Sebastiani (ibid, p. 157):

> When diagnosing a chronic illness, the doctor will certainly, unless it is best to do so, present the patient with facts that will shake up their life and their self-concepts. Being chronically ill means fighting against your ever-increasing disabilities; it's much more difficult than adapting

to an acute illness that only requires a temporary acceptance of passivity and external help.

So, even though it is very difficult for the patient, it is necessary for him to reorganize his life, restructuring it, due to his illness that implies some limitations and losses, including autonomy. Lifestyles change, diet changes, work life is often interrupted, medication and treatment necessarily become part of daily life, and adaptation to this new way of living is essential.

In addition, the chronicity of the illness and its permanent treatment make the patient dependent on the hospital, since going there to treat their illness becomes a routine that in some cases can occur more than once a week. The future, in turn, becomes hazy and anxiety-producing, because even if the patient is rigorously committed to the treatment, there are factors that can occur over time, due to organ weakness.

Each chronic disease has specific treatments, which cause symptoms that are characteristic of that pathology, for example, chronic kidney disease, which in its initial phase of treatment of hemodialysis sessions, the patient feels tired, apathetic, nauseous, weak and without any physical disposition.

It is therefore essential that the hospital psychologist distinguishes between the symptoms of the illness and the psychological symptoms in relation to it, because medicine deals with the organic symptoms, while psychology deals with the emotional aspects of the patient that occur as a result of their illness.

In this way, Cesarino and Casagrande (1998) also postulate that the patient's personal, family and social life is affected not only by the physical aspect, but also by the psychological situation arising from the patient's pathology, as well as the hemodialysis treatment.

Faced with this, there is a feeling of fear, anguish and a series of future uncertainties. Thus, hospital psychology is there to help the patient get through each stage.

Therefore, Simonetti's (2013, p.20) statement is pertinent when he states that:

> Hospital psychology could never work from a philosophy of healing, firstly because it proposes to deal with situations in which healing is no longer possible, such as chronic and terminal illnesses, and secondly because as a healing technology, in the medical sense of eradicating illnesses and eliminating symptoms, psychology is very inefficient. The psychologist can do very little in relation to the illness itself - this is the doctor's job - but he can do a lot in terms of the patient's relationship with his symptom: this is the psychologist's job.

Therefore, the doctor works with the physical body and the organic pathology, the psychologist works with the patient's speech, willing to listen to what they have to say, and even if they talk about their physical pain, behind this report is the subjectivity of dealing with this pain.

Knowing that each patient is affected by their life history, culture and also their beliefs, these factors interfere in the way they deal with their illness, their illness and subsequently the treatment required for their pathology. Thus, this subjectivity, laden with these crossings, needs to be heard, because during this patient's speech, the way he experiences this experience comes out. It is in saying how painful and difficult it is for him to be in this situation that his repressed materials will emerge.

Therefore, Alberti (2008, p. 158) states that:

> If, first and foremost, the patient is a subject, it is because they have a history that involves the rags that have marked their life since early childhood, and which are absolutely unique to them, just as we can say that fingerprints are unique from the point of view of forensic medicine. In order to have access to this subject, it is necessary for him to speak, which is the only way to know him, the only way for him to know himself, to the point where we can define the subject as the one who speaks. [...]

Corroborating this statement, just as fingerprints are unique, each subject is unique in their interactions and ways of coping, including with their illness, their disease and their symptom, therefore, it is from speech that subjectivity manifests itself, showing how the relationship occurs with what they feel in the face of pain, treatment, the impediments arising from their chronic illness.

Thus, it is by listening to this patient, who is in pain and sometimes doesn't accept medical treatment, presenting resistance, and this condition is unbearable for him, that the psychologist, based on the clinic, works in the hospital. However, it is necessary to know how to listen to the subjectivity of this suffering subject, because what matters is what the patient does with his symptom, which is known through language, that is, the word.

3 HOSPITAL PSYCHOLOGY BASED ON PSYCHOANALYSIS

The work of hospital psychologists must be supported by a theoretical approach that underpins their practice in this context. Psychoanalysis has therefore been one of the important approaches used as a basis for psychological care in hospital.

However, there is still a certain obscurity on the part of other health professionals regarding the use of psychoanalytic approaches and techniques in hospital, based on the premise that psychoanalysis is a time-consuming form of care, referring to the idea that it is only possible in conventionally known consulting rooms.

3.1 PSYCHOANALYSIS IN HOSPITAL

The presence of psychoanalysis in the hospital is pertinent, as it is nothing more than a return to its place of origin, where Freud sought to understand hysterical phenomena, as Moretto (2002) states. However, there are some obstacles and one of them is still the misconception about the role of psychoanalysis in the hospital.

Therefore, today we are trying to reconcile psychoanalysis with the hospital and, since the hospital is still dominated by doctors, we need to overcome some misconceptions on the part of doctors and other health professionals with whom they will necessarily have to deal during their daily practice. After all, there are still questions about what psychoanalysis actually is and how it works in the hospital.

In this sense, it's worth saying that in hospital, there are sometimes misconceptions on the part of the healthcare team regarding the work of psychology, which, for example, lead them to see the hospital psychologist as someone who will eliminate the patient's anguish, as Moretto (2002, p.21) states:

> Once the institution's demands had been determined, they were to calm down, to eliminate any kind of anguish that was circulating in the air, to convince patients of something that had not yet been achieved, to help whoever was falling.

However, the hospital psychologist makes the most of the door that has been opened to him, always guided by ethics, taking care not to detract from his place, his clinical practice and his important role in this area, where medicine dominates, because sometimes what the hospital psychologist is asked to do is to convince the patient of something they don't want, since it is not the health team's job to understand the reason for the patient's distress.

This is the difficult task of the hospital psychologist, who is not there to extinguish anguish or convince the patient of anything, but to listen to the patient in order to minimize their suffering. However, even with its obstacles, this is not an impossible task, and the inclusion of this psychoanalytically-based professional in this space is becoming more and more common.

However, there are still paradigms that refer to psychoanalysis as only being appropriate in the consulting room, which prevents it from being seen as an approach to psychology that joins other knowledge in the hospital field, not just being practiced by one more health professional, but that this professional performs his role with the team, helping the patient to deal with his illness in a less painful way.

On psychoanalytic work in hospital, Nogueira (1993) apud

Catani (2013, p.28) postulates that:

> We don't adopt any kind of framework a priori, because it is built together with the patient in order to provide an evolutionary process, in which the person being analyzed gradually lets go of rules that, at first,

> were impossible to disregard. There is a change that accompanies the expressions of the transferential relationship, and also to the extent that the subject becomes more organized and can therefore break away from established patterns, towards a particular construction that includes the subjectivity of the analysand.

There is, therefore, no rule to which psychoanalysis is strictly subject in terms of its practice in the hospital, as this is something that has to be built up with the patient over the course of the appointments, so that their subjectivity is possible through speech.

However, with the expansion of this practice into other spheres, psychoanalysis has slowly been making inroads, showing possibilities for effective intervention. This practice embraces clinical practice, but not entirely, because this non-traditional space is a place of creation, in which there is a relationship with other professionals in an interdisciplinary way. Thus, we have the notion of an extended clinic, which goes beyond a limited physical space and which, according to Campos (2012, p.34), can be understood as:

> [...] a notion that encompasses the practices of clinical care in the field of psychology that do not take place within the historically and epistemologically consolidated space of the classic consulting room. In other words, they are not totally inscribed in the model of the private consulting room, and are not totally "protected" by consolidated clinical knowledge, established theories and physical and spatial conditions under the control of the psychologist.

Still according to the same author (ibid), it is in practices beyond the four-walled space that the notion of an expanded clinic is most clearly defined, since social clinic consultations still reproduce the same model as traditionally known consultations.

The expansion of clinical practice has increasingly reached other areas, such as general hospitals, for example, and this is due to the recognition of the importance of psychological care for patients who are hospitalized or undergoing treatment.

Therefore, according to Lazzaretti (2007), Hospital Psychology is understood as an offshoot of clinical psychology in hospital institutions. The approach to subjectivity, a specific characteristic of human beings, can take place in any context of their lives in which they find themselves.

This statement makes it clear that regardless of where the subject is, it is possible to approach them and develop a therapeutic work from there, because what is wanted is to treat what is not palpable, that is, what is of the psychic order and for this, as long as the subject is willing to talk about their anguish, psychological care takes place.

Thus, Elias (2008, p. 88) states that:

> The psychoanalytic clinic, consecrated as a practice carried out in consulting rooms, has its paradox in the verb clinicar: it means bedside care. Freud was a doctor and, when he began his first experiments into the psyche with hysterics, he demonstrated how the hospital can be a fertile space for observing the human subject in the face of what affects them the most: their psychic fragility affected by a somatic event that is irremediably inscribed in the field of speech and language.

In addition, Freud, in his text Lines of progress in psychoanalytic therapy, had already predicted other spheres in which psychoanalysis would operate, since its beginnings were in hospital institutions and it is now possible to contemplate this statement in practice, when hospital psychologists provide care based on this approach, bringing a view that highlights the subjectivity of the same patient that medicine treats.

Thus, Freud (1919 [1918] 2006, p.180) in his text aforementioned, then postulates:

> Let's assume that, through some kind of organization, we manage to increase our numbers sufficiently to treat a considerable mass of the population. [There will be institutes or clinics for out-patients, to which analytically trained doctors will be assigned, so that men who would otherwise give in to drink, women who have practically succumbed to their burden of privates, children for whom there is no choice but

> brutalization or neurosis, may become capable, through analysis, of endurance and efficient work. [...] It may be a long time before the state comes to understand how urgent these duties are. [...] Sooner or later, however, we will. We will then be faced with the task of adapting our technique to the new conditions.

However, working with psychoanalysis in hospital requires a different approach to that of a consultant in terms of time, setting and the meaning of the symptom, which is different for medicine because it doesn't see it with the same eyes as psychology, because while the former locates the place where it manifests in the physical body, the latter finds it in the symbolic body, which is nowhere else but in the patient's words.

Thus, for Moretto (2002, p. 85 - 87):

> In the field of medicine, the symptom, even if it is presented by the patient, is constituted by the doctor. [...] In the field of psychoanalysis, it's not a question of overcoming symptoms, but of interpreting them. [...] The psychoanalytic symptom only exists as long as it is spoken by the patient, in other words, the psychoanalytic clinic is fundamentally a clinic made by patients, originating from their own discourse.

However, when it comes to the subject's quality of life, the two tend to complement each other, even if the way of looking at the subject is different, as is the way of intervening, because what we want is a dialogue between the two, not privileging one or the other, but emphasizing the importance of both. Therefore, it is possible to do clinical work in the hospital, because the effectiveness of psychoanalytic practice in the hospital exists, is recognized and makes it subsist, even in the face of the challenges it has faced since its beginnings. This can be seen when the medical team notices that the patient is less anxious, accepting their treatment better and not showing so much resistance to the hospital routine, but it is a recognition to be won over time, showing its importance, its value and that it can contribute greatly to better health conditions for the patient.

In line with this, Lazzareti (2007, p.39) states that:

> Since their inception, psychoanalysts have worked in hospitals. In

> Brazil, this entry was somewhat belated as a place of work; more specifically, it came about with the great spread of psychoanalysis in the country from the 70s onwards. With mistakes and successes, they have opened doors and windows, built paths and sometimes bridges.

In view of this statement, it is essential to declare that the advance of technology, culture and science, as well as medicine, among other factors, affects the subjectivity of each individual in dealing with their pain and illness, and this fact requires psychologists working in hospitals not to be isolated in an established pattern, plastered in an immutable model, with no intention of updating or improving their knowledge. Therefore, it is necessary to know in order to understand and accompany the changes that have taken place over the years and to rethink your practice so that the patient who is suffering due to their illness, living with this new information including about their pathology, is welcomed in the best possible way.

So, says Mohallem (2003, p.25):

> [...] psychoanalysis is changing in order to help the subject deal with their suffering [...] We are in a time when life is demanding new arrangements. We see the phenomenology of the clinic changing as a result of the advances of culture. We see symptoms presenting themselves in new guises, we see new ways of manifesting suffering.

In this way, the path that psychoanalytic-based hospital psychology has taken over the years is precisely demonstrating its importance through the possibility of treating what is unbearable for the patient, because this approach works with the perspective of betting on the other as a subject through the speech of this person who has had their life crossed by physical pain, by organic discomfort, by losing his autonomy and necessarily reorganizing his life in order to deal with his suffering, which causes psychic symptoms, and these also deserve attention from the person who is qualified to listen to the anguish behind the subject's words, that is, the psychologist.

3.1.1 Setting

When we talk about psychoanalysis in hospitals, it is inevitable that we talk about the hospital setting, i.e. the place where the patient who is hospitalized or undergoing treatment is cared for, because it differs greatly from the conventional clinic, in terms of the delimited physical space and the tranquility of the appointments without the noise and/or interruptions that are characteristic of a hospital.

Thus, for Moretto (2001, p.59) "[...] We cannot be dealing with the setting as a real space because it is virtual, it is psychic, it

It is, in fact, an artifice, a construction by the psychoanalyst so that the analysis can take place".

Each sector of the hospital has its own daily routine, some of which can be quieter, others not so much. In the setting, there isn't total privacy during the psychological care of the patient, as there will always be procedures to be carried out on the patient, such as: checking blood pressure, glucose, administering medication, changing access points, among others, and also remembering that there is always another health professional around. However, none of these factors can compromise psychological care, because it is necessary to create this space, this place, without allowing external interference to hinder clinical practice.

Corroborating this statement, Simonetti (2013, p.156)

argues that:

> One of the reasons for the success that psychology has achieved on the hospital scene is that it needs very little to work: all it takes is a subject who wants to talk and a psychologist who knows how to listen, and the rest is an accessory. Inadequate location, lack of privacy, noise, interruptions, short time, discredit from other members of the team, etc., all of this can be solved, it's not fundamental.

Therefore, it is the subjectivity of the suffering subject, the way they deal with their illness and their symptoms, that is of interest to psychoanalysis in hospital. This, however, takes place through speech, which manifests its unconscious contents, laden with crossings other than just its illness.

Therefore, there is no standard to be followed when it comes to the setting, as it is possible to practice psychoanalytic psychology in the hospital, demystifying misconceptions about this work.

To this end, Moretto (2002) states that the only rule left by Freud, called the "golden rule", was free association.

Therefore, according to the same author (ibid, p. 59):

> The contract with psychoanalysis is based on the fundamental rule: the rest is perfumery, the rest is the rest. What is contracted in psychoanalysis is the following: the patient associates freely, and the analyst pays fluctuating attention. This is the contract, this is the commitment between patient and analyst, because it is only in this setting that we can think about resistance, the establishment of transference and the possibilities of analytical intervention.

In this way, the hospital psychologist is there to listen and know how to listen, because listening is their main working tool, leading the patient towards the word and what is heard from the patient is not just words, but a speech full of subjectivity that in a unique way expresses the pain and anguish that now prevents them from having their autonomy and being seen as a subject, needing to be heard on their issues.

Therefore, psychoanalysis works with the unconscious, in order to bring out the material that is there and this occurs through the patient's speech, made possible through free association, that is, the patient is allowed to talk about what comes to mind and this is the fundamental rule of psychoanalytic theory.

Confirming this, Freud ([1913] 2006, p.149) postulates that:

> The material with which the treatment begins is generally indifferent - the patient's life story, or the story of their illness, or their childhood memories. But in all cases, the patient should be allowed to speak and should be free to choose where to start. In this way, we tell them: 'Before I can tell you anything, I need to know a lot about you; please tell me what you know about yourself'.

The method of free association, therefore, was adopted by Freud after he abandoned hypnosis when he realized that it wasn't as effective, because when the patient came out of the hypnotic state, he couldn't remember what he had said during the process. Freud then realized that allowing the patient to talk about themselves was the best way to reach the repressed contents. Thus, according to Jorge and Ferreira (2010, p.38):

> From the cathartic method to free association, Freud discovers another scene beyond consciousness, which is the unconscious. The method of free association consists of summoning the analysand to say what they feel and what they think, without the interference of any process of choice or moral judgment.

Simonetti (2013, p.117) states that "This invitation to speak freely must be matched by free listening on the part of the psychologist". This means, then, that the patient must be listened to without there being a selection of his or her speech, in other words, we must listen to exactly everything the patient says, which will not always be only about his or her illness. Therefore, we shouldn't prioritize one part or another of the patient's story, because during their free speech, without punctuation, and in some cases they may be disconnected or not follow an order when speaking, unconscious content that the patient themselves doesn't realize they are saying will emerge, being very important in order to arrive at the meaning that the illness has for them and what their relationship is with this fact that distresses them.

In his text: Recommendations for doctors practicing psychoanalysis, Freud ([1912] 2006, p. 125 - 126) states that:

> The technique, however, is very simple: [...] It simply consists of not

> directing your attention to something specific and maintaining the same 'uniformly suspended attention' (as I have called it) in the face of everything you hear. In this way, we save our attention from violent effort, which in any case could not be maintained for several hours every day, and we avoid a danger that is inseparable from the exercise of deliberate attention.

Still in the same text, Freud postulates that a very centralized attention selects the content that has been reported by the patient, and that some parts may be fixed in the analyst's memory, but others may not, and that this "follows the expectations and inclinations" of the analyst. He goes on to say that: "This, however, is exactly what should not be done. [...] it should not be forgotten that what is heard, for the most part, are things whose meaning is only identified later."

In this way, having an attention span that is too centralized hinders the understanding of what the patient says, which will only occur a posteriori, when the meanings of this speech will be identified.

3.2 THE CLINICAL ENCOUNTER

The clinic within the hospital, as we have already discussed, is a practice that transcends space and place, because these are created from the patient's speech, after being offered a listening ear. Therefore, it is worth pointing out that one of the challenges faced by hospital psychologists is that it is not always the patient who has called them there, but this call may have come from another health professional, a hospital employee or even a relative of the patient, as Simonetti (2013, p.96) states:

> [...] a distinction should be made between a request for psychological care and a demand for psychological care. A request is a request for the hospital psychologist to see someone, and this request can be made by the patient, the doctor, the nurses or the family. The demand is a psychological state characterized by a questioning or discomfort, on the part of the person themselves, in relation to the way they are experiencing their illness, necessarily implying the existence of a certain level of psychic work. The request is an action, the demand a

state, which is why one person can request care on behalf of another, but no one can demand on behalf of another. The demand is always one's own.

Therefore, when the patient makes their own request, it means that they recognize that they are unable to cope with their suffering and therefore need a professional to help them through this time of pain. However, if someone else has requested psychological assistance, it won't be surprising if the patient receives the psychologist in a hostile manner.

However, when the psychologist introduces himself to the patient, he realizes that there is a professional there to listen to him, without judgment, without imposing medical procedures on him. Thus, everything is heard, because some patients bring issues from their childhood, others have never been hospitalized before and, from this speech, the deepest and most distressing way of dealing with their illness emerges. It's an encounter with oneself through speech, in the face of a biologically fragile situation.

Almost always, when this encounter takes place, the patient has already been informed of their pathology and its progression, in other words, the doctor has already given them an organic diagnosis. However, this diagnosis differs from the one that the hospital psychologist sets out to make with a broad view of what appears during the patient's speech and only then is it possible to interpret the meaning of the illness for him. Because subjectivity is complex and the symptom for psychology does not have a physical location, this reaction diagnosis is based on hypothesis and not absolute certainty, because these are psychic phenomena, manifested due to the suffering surrounding the physical illness.

Thus, with regard to diagnosis, according to Simonetti (2013, p. 33): In medicine, diagnosis is the knowledge of the illness through its symptoms, while in hospital psychology diagnosis is the knowledge of the existential and subjective situation of the sick person in their relationship with the illness. [...] We don't offer labels, but a panoramic view. [...] Diagnosis is the psychologist's way of organizing his thinking. [...] The diagnosis is a hypothesis, not an absolute truth. [...] The psychologist works with the meaning of things, not with the truth of things.

Each patient, therefore, reacts differently to becoming ill; the same illness is faced in a particular way according to each individual, because given the subjectivity and uniqueness of each subject, this directs the forms of reaction, regardless of the pathology diagnosed by the doctor. This is how Simonetti (2013) confirms it, when he proposes in his Manual that the reaction diagnosis is the person's way of reacting to the illness and the medical diagnosis is the biological condition attested to by the doctor himself.

Regarding these two diagnoses, one differs from the other, mainly due to the fact that the medical diagnosis is invasive, through examination procedures, while the reactive diagnosis comes from the patient's words and way of behaving when faced with the news about their pathology. Therefore, given the particularity of each individual, the hospital psychologist should not expect patients suffering from the same pathology, for example, to behave in the same way, even in the face of the characteristic symptoms of the disease, because each one brings with them their own history, culture and even their own beliefs in the face of this new life condition.

Simonetti (ibid) also postulates that there is no difference between diagnosis and therapy, because when data is collected from the patient in order to make a diagnosis, therapy is already taking place. He also adds that the patient, in an orbit, at first denies the illness, not believing in what is unexpected in his life; then he rebels when he is faced with the reality of his illness, addressing this rebellion to others or even to himself and the illness; then he goes into a depressive state, in a passive position, disbelieving in the treatment and consequently in the cure for his illness; and finally, the confrontation of reality, not deluding himself, when he has already gone through the other positions. As far as this is concerned, there is no right order for these positions and the patient can fixate on one of them, but it is not immutable and they can change position every day.

It is well known, then, that the process of hospitalization or hospital treatment means that the patient's organic condition is not performing its functions in a healthy way, thus indicating that their health is somehow impaired. In many cases of patients undergoing hospitalization and/or treatment, the diagnosis is to confirm that something serious is happening and, consequently, the prognosis is not encouraging, as some patients may not have long to live or may depend on a specific treatment to ensure their survival. These issues are closely linked to the idea of death, which brings with it a feeling of dread and intense fear on the part of those who have a diagnosis attesting to damage, in many cases severe damage to their health. Thus, Kubler-Ross (1996, p. 14) states that:

> [...] In our unconscious, death is never possible when it comes to ourselves. It is inconceivable for the unconscious to imagine a real end to our life on earth and, if life does come to an end, it will always be attributed to an evil intervention beyond our reach. [...] So death itself is linked to an evil deed, to a dreadful event, to something that in itself cries out for reward or punishment.

Faced with this, the patient sees himself as powerless over his biological condition, and is then dependent on science and medicine, because man only realizes that there is a real body the moment it falls ill and threatens his existence. Freud ([1915] 2006, p. 303) states that: "For early man, his own death was certainly as unimaginable and unreal as it is for any of us today." [...]

Thus, for Soares (1999, p.106):

> The human body, in its perfect functioning, comes to us with a harmonious physiology, where the systems and apparatus of the human machine interact, making it possible for death to be an event for the distant future. However, the only prediction we have of life is death. Faced with this prediction, projects are sought to maintain life. These projects tell us, then, that this body contradicts the ideal perfection of functioning and that something, present in its constitution, fails and escapes man's control.

This organ fragility frightens the patient, affecting their psychic ability to deal with this situation. Thus, Kubler-Ross (1996) postulates on the stages that patients go through when faced with a serious pathology and/or a short life prognosis: denial and isolation, anger, bargaining, depression and acceptance. These stages are in no particular order and not everyone necessarily goes through all of them.

It is in the face of these reappraisals, and going through some of the phases mentioned above, that the hospital psychologist will encounter the subjectivity of the patient who is hospitalized or undergoing treatment, which is a very common reason for being asked to provide psychological care.

We should therefore return to the concept of psychoanalysis, which is interested in the unconscious as manifested through speech. The following is Freud's concept (1919[1918] 2006, p. 173)
when he states: "We call psychoanalysis the process by which we bring repressed mental material into the consciousness of the patient". This is then a process that takes place through the patient's speech, and this only occurs through the established bond, that is, the transference.

In this respect, Freud ([1914] 2006, p.170) states:

> [...] The transference thus creates an intermediate region between the illness and real life, through which the transition from one to the other takes place. The new condition has taken on all the characteristics of the illness, but it represents an artificial illness, which is in every respect accessible to our intervention. [...]

The transference in hospital, a priori, is not with the psychologist but with the doctor, who in turn turns to the physical body. So, the patient wants to know about his pathology from the doctor, given the idea that the doctor knows everything about his illness and has the answers to it. The hospital psychologist, on the other hand, is interested in the subject, in the relationship they have with their symptom, and is willing to listen, with the aim of enabling the patient to deal with their issues in the least painful and distressing way possible.

In this way, Simonetti (2015, p.188) states:

> The patient's transference is with the doctor, but it is the analyst who presents himself. It's a big mismatch: the patient wants to talk, the analyst wants to listen, but the patient wants to be listened to by the doctor, who doesn't want to know anything other than what interests him, but which he recognizes is important to the patient.[...]

Therefore, in this counterpoint to the hospital route, patients are offered their place as subjects to put into words the extent of their pain. Therefore, once this bond has been established, it is of great importance, but in the hospital environment, such can be the anguish of being hospitalized that it is unbearable for the patient to talk about their issues, at least at first.

Simonetti (2015, p. 183) states that: "[...] there are other situations in which patients lack words, not because of anatomical impairment, but because of the abrupt emergence of such anguish that it cannot be expressed in words." Therefore, the patient may not want to talk at first or even after a few sessions.

Thus, even if the patient is unable to put their feelings of anguish into words, their silence must be heard and welcomed, because silence is also a way of expressing themselves, and this will also bring to light their unique way of getting through the current situation in which they live by confronting what ails them, which is a factor that requires time. This time must be patiently waited for, until the subject is able to verbalize what they feel, in the midst of the pathological chaos they have been affected by.

This is then the moment to welcome this subject with silence, respecting this moment of such pain that it is impossible to put into words, but being willing to listen to him, whenever he wishes, because for Simonetti (2013, p. 116): "The psychologist wants the patient to speak because he believes that by speaking he symbolizes his suffering and dissolves his anguish. Anguish is not resolved, it is dissolved in words".

3.2.1 Time

Time is also a very pertinent issue in the work of hospital psychologists, because when people talk about the psychoanalytic approach, they immediately think of analysis, in other words, a long period of psychological care, leading to misconceptions about this work in hospital, since the hospitalization and consequently the psychological care will end mainly when the patient is discharged. However, psychoanalysis in hospital works in a way that is adapted to this context, with the subject's time.

It should also be said that, even if the patient has been discharged and returns to hospital, the psychological care they receive from then on will be new, as they will be at a different time, expressing their subjectivity in relation to what they are facing again.
About this time, Oliveira (2003, pg. 47 - 48) states that:

> So many times, in a hospital, we provide care distributed over time in a way that would be unthinkable in a clinic. So many times we receive the discourse of the same patient in successive hospitalizations, where each discursive occasion is different from the previous ones. [...] The times of each subject... There is not just one time in action. It would be better to speak of times. The plural takes us away from the common linear, sequential notion, where facts are ordered in an inevitable cause and effect relationship.

Time, therefore, depends on each subject, each service, the management that needs to be done, what is urgent for that service to be carried out. There is no set time for each treatment, as far as its duration is concerned. What we do have is a time that we only know when we are in front of the patient, even for those who have been hospitalized for several months or are undergoing a long course of treatment, as in the case of chronic patients.

In the hospital, time is fast, as the doctor is in a hurry to act because the patient is at risk. On the other hand, the patient's time is different, because it is based on their subjectivity, and each person has their own time to understand what is happening.

Therefore, as Simonetti (2015, p. 198 - 199) states: "The doctor is in a hurry, he needs to act quickly, because life is in danger; the subject, on the other hand, needs time, in every sense, he wants more time to live, and he needs time to work through the beatings that life gives him, especially that of becoming ill."

Thus, with regard to chronic patients who are hospitalized or undergoing treatment in hospital, there is more time to work with them, as the psychologist will have more encounters with them than with a patient suffering from an acute illness, which may even occur more than once a week. Even so, this patient will bring new issues to psychological care, not least because of the chronicity of their illness, which is something very difficult to deal with, as it is not just a moment that the subject is trying to get through, but a new condition of life that now needs to be adapted to their daily lives.

3.3 THE WILLIAM CASE

A supermarket stockist, married for around 8 months, William, at 21, is the father of a 3-year-old boy, the fruit of a relationship prior to marriage. According to the information we have gathered, he is "a chronic patient" in the hemodialysis sector, where "the almost total paralysis of his two kidneys occurred due to arterial hypertension". As this condition attracted attention due to its seriousness, the fact that he was a young patient and that he cried a lot, the health team asked psychology to pay attention to William's case.

When he was seen by the psychology service, William was able to put the extent of his suffering into words. He told us that he had a headache and didn't mind it because he didn't he used to go to the doctor, but on his mother's advice, he went for a medical consultation, where he was diagnosed with hereditary hypertension.

According to his account, William didn't administer the prescribed medication correctly, he took the medication when he wanted and if he wanted, because he considered himself to be "irresponsible" and "inconsequential" and didn't take care of his health. He said: *"I'm here doing hemodialysis because I was irresponsible."* As a result, his situation worsened, and on one occasion he felt unwell and was hospitalized for a few days at the UPA (Emergency Care Unit), where he was referred to a nephrologist to begin hemodialysis treatment.

According to her account, this news and the beginning of the treatment, especially the first few days, were "the most terrible, frightening and worrying", because she didn't know what it was all about.

It's well known that when you start hemodialysis, you feel very discouraged, apathetic and somewhat unwilling to do anything. In this way, the patient reported that he *"couldn't leave the house anymore, saying that his head said one thing, but his body said another", in other* words, there was a desire to move around, go out, go for a walk, visit relatives and friends, etc., but his physical condition prevented it.

From the first appointment, the patient said that he had overcome the situation he was now experiencing in relation to his hemodialysis treatment, but when asked to talk about it, he said: *"Actually, I haven't overcome it, but I have accepted this situation. There's no way, I have to come for treatment. I*

have this treatment as a job, I come here three times a week to work for four hours a day. At work and in the barracks I had timetables and rules, here it's the same. Every day I think about 45
not come. When I think about coming here I feel discouraged, but I have to, there's no way. "

Over the course of the appointments, William, who at first spoke very little, is now able to elaborate on his questions, talking about his life before treatment, when he went out with friends, worked, played soccer, etc. and about his future plans, including his working life.

William also told us about what happened in his childhood, as well as his relationship with his father and stepfather, saying that "they weren't very good, and he wasn't very close to his father". He said: *"I lived with my mother and my stepfather from the time I was four (4) years old. My stepfather was always very strict and demanded that I study, forbade me to go out, grounded me and I was already a teenager. One day I couldn't stand it and I left home and moved out on my own.* The patient also said that his illness had brought him closer to his biological father and that he now lives very close to him.

At the beginning of the appointments, William was always on the phone, talking to his wife or listening to music with his headphones on, but whenever I arrived in the hemodialysis department and approached, the patient would remove his headphones and if he was talking to his wife, he would turn them off and turn his attention to me.

After a few visits, a nurse commented that William "didn't speak, but now he was talking and interacting with other people". I was also able to observe that William was sometimes already talking to the nurses before the psychological care began, which was not the case at the beginning.

In view of the above, it was also possible to observe how the patient behaves in the face of any intercurrence in his treatment, such as when he feels pain at the access site and also when it is not possible to use the same fistula and a new procedure has to be performed. I stayed close to William throughout this process and, at certain moments, he would look at me, pale, with an expression of pain, holding his arm very tightly, squeezing it, enduring the physical pain and also the anguish of the possibility of a new surgical intervention to change the fistula if it could no longer be used. Meanwhile, the nurse asked him if he had taken care of his arm properly, as instructed. At the end of this process, I approached William and asked him if he wanted to say anything and his answer was "no", in a gestural way, shaking his head, without saying a word.

The health team then perceives him as "fearful" due to the way William behaves in the face of adverse situations arising from his treatment, when he complains of physical pain resulting from some intercurrence and the few times the patient missed treatment were also understood by the team as if he was not involved with his treatment.

We also had the opportunity to see the patient before he started his treatment (hemodialysis session), in a different setting, in a separate room, where he felt more at ease during the psychological treatment, and even told us about his anxiety regarding the waiting time before starting dialysis, especially when there was a delay in starting. William said: *"I always arrive on time, but they always delay my start time. I think this is a lack of responsibility, because the longer I take to start, the later I have to leave, to make up for the delay."*

One day, when he arrived at the hemodialysis ward to see William, he was anxious because he had to be hospitalized due to an infection in his fistula, which could cause further damage to his health. The patient then reported that he couldn't eat, because his mouth was very sore, due to the reaction to the antibiotic he had been prescribed, adding: *"I feel very alone here, I can't go home, I only see my wife during visiting hours, I have no one to talk to". [sic]*

For their part, the health team told William to eat, as his body would react better to the medication and he would be discharged more quickly. The patient stayed in hospital for a few days, just long enough for the infection to stop. At his next appointment, William was looking better and at the end of it, the doctor approached him to announce that he would be discharged from hospital the following day.

When faced with the possibility of being transplanted, William began to allow something of himself to appear beyond the dialysis scene. Even though he was aware of the possible rejection, as well as the waiting time, which could be months or years, William managed to reposition himself in the face of his suffering. The desire "to get rid of the dialysis machine" gave way to the possibility of pianos for the future, however uncertain.

He has been able to recapture a part of his life before he fell ill, has started going out with friends and his wife, and is still planning something to do with work.

William, in a situation of complete dependence, can put himself in another place, since he has presented his plans to get his own business, "a pizzeria, not to have a lot of money to save but to spend, to buy his things" and thus get on with his life.

4 CASE DISCUSSION

The organic impairment leads the subject to psychically manifest their way of living and dealing with this situation in a peculiar way, as there is a break with their way of life in various aspects. As this is a chronic illness, for which there is no cure, the patient learns to live with something permanent, i.e. treatment, which becomes part of their routine, necessarily for many years or even for the rest of their life.

Chronic nephropathic patients, i.e. those suffering from chronic renal failure, are literally dependent on the dialysis machine, which replaces their kidneys once they are no longer fully functional. This often causes patients in the early stages of treatment to become depressed due to their fear of the unknown and even the risk of death, their loss of autonomy and the care they must take with their health through food and prescribed medication.

Therefore, the patient goes through a whirlwind of organic and emotional issues, needing to adjust to a new life routine, as a way of contributing to their treatment, so that there is quality of life and, consequently, guarantees their survival. Treatment depends indispensably on the active and effective participation of each patient, as they make a commitment to themselves and their health, enabling a good prognosis for life.

It is important to discuss the use of and difference between a catheter and an arteriovenous fistula, and in this case the patient in question was dialyzed for the first few days via a catheter, usually placed in the neck or groin, a process that was carried out via microsurgery. The catheter is used in such a way that it is exposed to the body and must be cared for as hygienically as possible so that it does not become infected and cause complications to the patient's health.

According to information gathered in the hemodialysis department, at first, the patient used a catheter until he had his registration, that is, his medical record in the SUS (Sistema Unico de Saude) and then the catheter was replaced by the fistula, which is an arteriovenous access in two (2) arteries, allowing blood to enter and leave the patient's body simultaneously, passing through the hemodialysis machine, filtering (cleaning) the blood.

The fistula, unlike the catheter, is under the patient's skin and is also placed via microsurgery, but does not appear externally. However, the patient must take the same care to avoid causing infections and jeopardizing his health and treatment. All the necessary instructions for the patient's self-care are given by the health team.

Thus, in the face of these necessary interventions, the patient's body bears the mark of their treatment, as the fistula scar is visible and the skin changes its color after a while. Brant (1999, p.89) then states that: "[...] The patient's body is aggressively marked by edema, fistula scars, cuts for catheter insertion [...]"

In addition to undergoing hemodialysis treatment, which causes discouraging reactions in the patient, especially making their interpersonal relationships difficult, they must also eat a healthy, fat-free diet to avoid gaining weight so that the treatment is effective, and they must also avoid drinking too much water, since their kidneys no longer carry out the natural process of filtering the blood. Blood pressure must be regulated with the prescribed medication and the fistula must be well looked after so that it doesn't become infected or damaged. These are, therefore, the basics of care so that the patient can have the quality of life necessary to guarantee their health and survival.

Brant (ibid, p. 90) says of these aspects:

> From a social and emotional point of view, these patients' relationships become conflictive, given the limitations to which they are condemned. Limitations ranging from food and fluid intake to sexual impotence.

Patients also receive a benefit from the INSS (National Institute of Social Security), once the chronic illness is proven and they are no longer able to continue working, and free public transport tickets are also part of the benefits received.

Thus, from a biopsychosocial perspective, the chronic nephropathic patient is faced with various issues, including his inability to continue his working life, so he has to find other solutions for an abrupt reorganization of his life in all its aspects. To this end, hospital psychology contributes greatly to this process of personal, social, affective and emotional change and rearrangement, helping patients to cope with and reposition themselves in this new way of living. Together, the patient and the hospital psychologist build a bond that is indispensable for the effectiveness of getting through the pain and anguish of this atrocious event for the patient.

The patient's care was never free from interruptions for medical procedures and noises, including beeps from the dialyzer machine. However, the patient was always attentive to the psychological care, not interrupting his speech, even when a member of the health team approached to check his blood pressure, for example.

In view of this, throughout the appointments, the patient brought up personal and family factors, his previous jobs, his relationship with his parents, his wife, his son and what his life was like before treatment.

Thus, the first issue the patient faced was not knowing what the disease and the treatment were about, and these first days were "the most fearful". In this initial phase, the patient is unexpectedly confronted with his organ fragility, and is overwhelmed by intense crying during his first hemodialysis sessions.

Therefore, Freud ([1914] 2006, p. 168) states that:

> [...] The patient must find the courage to turn his attention to the phenomena of his illness. His illness itself must no longer seem contemptible to him, but must become an enemy worthy of his temper,

> a fragment of his personality, which has a solid foundation for existence and from which things of value for his future life must be inferred. [...]

Chronic illness consequently brings loss to the patient, with the first news of loss being that of their health, which causes the patient suffering. Therefore, for patients to be able to deal with this situation in a less distressing way, they first need to understand what is happening about the reality of their illness and also the issue of losing what they have always had, i.e. autonomy, social life and employment. This has a huge impact on the life of this person, who is now dependent on treatment, medication, medicine and other factors that favor their total well-being.

When the patient understands that this break in some aspects of their life is necessary, it enables them to cope better with the conditions that their chronic illness imposes on them.

Therefore, a priori, when the patient appropriates this place as an active subject, collaborating with the priority needs related to their treatment, they begin to experience mourning in reaction to a new unavoidable life condition, in other words, they begin to live in such a way as to refrain from what they can always do autonomously, due to the limitations of the disease, in favor of collaborating with their treatment.

Thus, according to Freud (1917[1915] 2006, p. 249): "[...] Mourning in general is the reaction to the loss of a loved one, the loss of some abstraction that has taken the place of a loved one, such as one's parents, one's freedom, or one's ideal, and so on [...]".

This abstraction, which has taken the place of their full autonomy, especially in the early stages, has the preponderant factor of learning to live in a very different way than before. Mourning now occupies a place previously filled by various other activities that the illness no longer allows. The first steps taken in beginning to mourn are the first steps towards a life with more rules, timetables and the impositions of the illness and treatment. They are the first steps towards change, and every change implies loss, which generates anguish and anxiety on the part of the patient.

The mourning phase, therefore, according to Simonetti (2013) is accompanied by sadness, due to the patient's inevitable losses and also a depressed state, as it is the beginning of this treatment and he is facing a new life condition that includes many changes. It was then possible to see that the patient's crying and his depressed state at the beginning were due to the essential losses he had to deal with.

Thus, when the patient reports that: "I couldn't leave the house anymore, saying that my head said one thing, but my body said another,
that he used to go out with his friends, work, play soccer with his friends and now he doesn't", it is possible to observe and identify the mourning that the patient has experienced in relation to the loss of a life that he now no longer lives as he used to, being unable to work due to the treatment, also affecting his social, emotional and other aspects. He now experiences a loss not only of physical health but also of the active life he used to have.

However, his desire to move around, enjoy a full social life, go for walks and work is preserved, not extinguished, even in the face of his weakened physical condition.

At the beginning of the sessions, William was still unable to cope well with this situation, mainly because of the discouragement and weakness that come with treatment, which was an obstacle to him being able to go out with his wife, for example. The mourning process, therefore, came about through the patient's speech, when he was given the opportunity to put his issues into words.

When he says that he has "accepted his illness and sees the treatment as a job, because there is no other way", this makes it clear that William is aware of what is happening to him, and that it is a moment of encounter with the reality of his illness, which causes changes in his life, as Freud ([1914] 2006, p. 167) states: "[...] the beginning of the treatment itself brings about a change in the patient's conscious attitude towards his illness. [...]", but this fact does not exempt them from the anguish and suffering related to their pathology and the treatment.

This change in conscious attitude is brought about by the manifestation of the unconscious through words, enabling the patient to overcome this initial moment of confrontation with their illness.

Therefore, according to Simonetti (2013), it is possible to perceive in this report the patient's coping position in 54
He was able to react to his illness by "alternating between the postures of struggle and mourning", facing his treatment as a new routine in his life.

Coping is a position in which the patient neither denies nor neglects their illness and treatment; on the contrary, it is a daily struggle that the patient strategically goes through, facing their new daily life, made up of mourning what they can no longer have. The subject goes to the limit in dealing with the chronicity of the illness, in an attempt to modify this condition and tries to bear the losses arising from this same biological condition.

Therefore, Simonetti (ibid, p.61) also states that: "Struggle is everything a person does in the face of a limit, trying to change it, and mourning is everything a person does in the face of an object loss, trying to bear it." In this position, the patient knows that they are free to take a stand and that it no longer matters why they are ill, but what to do from then on. This is a position in which nothing is being denied and the patient is powerful, even though they are ill. In this position, the patient then makes their subjectivity explicit, in a unique way, based on their response to the situation, which is a way out of dealing with this condition that is unbearable for them, in a true position.

Mohallem (2003, p. 29) states that: "The patient may come up against the limits of his vulnerability, his helplessness, but also, on the other hand, discover how much he may be able to bear, test his potential and find previously unimaginable ways out of his anguish."

Many patients are aware of their potential to withstand

unbearable only in extreme situations such as a serious illness. It is at this moment that they are faced with the psychic strategies they can use to cope with their pain. It is in the face of loss that the individual learns about their ability to live with what is distressing and terrible for them.

We can therefore see the importance of the patient's position in relation to his illness, fighting to contribute to his treatment, showing himself to be involved in this process that has totally changed his life, knowing his real health condition, including the risks, as Simonetti (2013, p.24) states, enabling the "subject to cross over the experience of illness".

The fact that William was able to put into words his suffering in relation to his illness and also to his treatment was due to the bond established, which enabled him to expose his feelings and the way he dealt with his pathology. Thus, from the moment he was offered a listening ear, the patient was able to elaborate on his issues through words, which Freud ([1926] 2006, p. 185) states: "[...] are a powerful instrument; they are the means by which we convey our feelings to others, our method of influencing other people. Words can do untold good and cause terrible wounds".

Through speech, the anguish is gradually diluted, reducing the patient's suffering caused by the disease, because when he speaks he expresses his pain, and all this psychic event, not being heard, without the opportunity to express in words what is happening to him, can interfere with the work of the health team in caring for the patient, because this professional does not always know how to deal with the anguish of this other, and therefore the psychological care given to the patient is important.

Therefore, if the hospital psychologist offers to listen so that the patient can minimize their suffering through speech, when these repressed contents

appear consciously, Simonetti (2013, p.
24) states that: "By listening, the psychologist 'holds' the patient's anguish long enough for him, the patient, to be able to submit it to the work of symbolic elaboration. [...]"

Sustaining the anguish for a while, therefore, enables the patient to dissolve this feeling through words, and gives the patient the conditions to reduce their pain by talking about their discomfort.

Throughout the appointments, family issues were also reported by the patient. Thus, in some appointments, he repeated what he had just reported, but as he repeated it, he remembered other issues, updating his report to bring new content about his life.

In his text Remember, Repeat and Elaborate ([1914] 2006, p. 166), Freud states that: "As long as the patient is under treatment, he cannot escape this compulsion to repeat; and in the end, we understand that this is his way of remembering." It was therefore possible to see how William remembers past events in his life, which are significant to him and this information is also important for the treatment, providing an interpretation of how the patient deals with other situations that occur in his life.

The memory that appeared in William's account, therefore, was about deciding to live alone, leaving the dependence of his mother and stepfather, when he was still a teenager, and the desire to open a pizzeria with his father, refers to the autonomy of life, not only financial, but also in relation to the dialysis machine and the treatment itself, when he reports "wanting to get rid of the machine".

It can be seen that for William, autonomy is something very important, which he is now trying to recover in a way that is fair to his illness, without interfering in his treatment and damaging his health.

It was then possible to understand the way in which William faces adverse situations in his life, no different from his chronic illness which requires a new living condition, to which he has now had to adapt, making it clear in his speech that no one else is responsible for this situation but himself and that, therefore, in the face of this cruel reality, there is only room so far for struggle and coping with his illness.

With regard to his son, William has always said that he respects the days when he can be with him, which is every 15 (fifteen) days, by court order, since the child's mother is not his current wife. Thus, it is clear that even in the face of a disease that biologically weakens him, the patient is always willing to be with his son, taking responsibility for him. This fact also shows the patient's active coping stance, when he doesn't give up what is rightfully his.

The setting, on the other hand, although not the most tranquil and does not guarantee privacy, has never prevented William from positioning himself and putting his issues into words during the psychological consultations. On the contrary, he always contributed effectively to each service, with the exception of one occasion when he didn't want to talk about what had happened, when there was an intercurrence with his fistula and there was a very long process until the health team managed to reverse the situation so that he could dialyze that day.

In this regard, it is important to describe William's behavior, which was one of literal coping with the situation, helping the nurse to carry out the procedure. Although the patient was visibly pale and frightened due to the pain and anguish of the situation, he showed an expression that nothing could

58

The patient was struggling to cooperate with the procedure and facing the situation so that it could be resolved in the best possible way.

Given this, William showed in practice how involved he is with his treatment and how he faces the most difficult and physically painful situations, including during the hemodialysis session. In this way, his struggle and coping with his treatment, and especially this situation, appeared beyond his words, which always said something about his position on his illness.

Another important fact is that William, whenever he needed to be absent, which happened only a few times during this period of care, tried to let the health team know, and was interested in the possibility of dialyzing the next day.

Therefore, William is aware of the risks and damage that can occur to his health when he stops taking the treatment, even for a day, since the consequences of not taking the treatment are swelling, malaise, high blood pressure, among other symptoms.

Although William had always helped to ensure that the psychological treatment took place satisfactorily, in another setting, in a separate room, where it was possible to see him on one occasion, the patient was more comfortable talking. This time, he complained about his treatment and the time it started.

Thus, it is understood that for William, everything should always go satisfactorily, without intercurrences, delays or any other situation that prevents him from taking his treatment.

The hospitalization the patient underwent gave him a feeling of loneliness, as he reported that "he felt alone in the ward", because "he had no one to talk to", "he didn't see people outside of visiting hours". This loneliness is yet another loss of autonomy for the patient, as he was prevented from leaving the hospital because something had happened that could have further damaged his health. The grief he now faces is related to moving around and going to the hospital just to have his treatment, then returning home. This was, therefore, yet another break in William's already adapted daily life, and he had to face yet another situation arising from an organic illness, even though this situation occurred in just a few days.

Therefore, William was offered the opportunity to listen at different times so that he could talk about each moment he had been through, because listening to the expression of the feelings of this other sufferer enables the patient to go through this difficult journey less distressed and better able to cope with his illness as a unique individual who, in his own way, finds ways to deal with this suffering. Jugend and JurKiewicz (2012, p. 15) therefore state that:

> [...] it is an opportunity to elaborate on experiences. It takes place through the patient's talking and the professional's listening, opening up a space for the patient to talk about what they unconsciously know about themselves. As he talks, he surprises himself with the effects on him of these events that he was unaware of, but which reveal part of his life and help him to elaborate and live with these events as a story.

However, given these facts, psychological care should not be limited, but should develop more and more, contributing effectively to minimizing the suffering of those who find themselves in this treatment process.

In this way, it is possible to see how William is coping with his condition in hemodialysis, being aware of his limitations, facing the daily mourning of his previous life and, at the same time, the struggle related to his treatment. This is a far cry from the health team's description of him as "fearful" due to his complaints of physical pain as a result of some intercurrence.

This invites us to take a different stance, since the health team's view and report doesn't always tell us what is really happening with the patient. Sometimes, what is reported does not match what is observed in relation to the patient.

The healthcare team is not characterized by understanding the anguish of the patient it treats. Thus, with their technical and objective work, they often fail to take into account the subjectivity of this suffering subject.

In this way, Simonetti (2013) states that listening to the patient's distress is not a service provided by other health professionals, precisely because they can't bear to see the patient's suffering, so they want to deny it.

Thus, referring to patients as "fearful" is a way of saying that they are unable to cope with their illness and its treatment, when in fact it is the healthcare team that is unable to bear the anguish of this other person who is not exempt from the care and physical interventions necessary for treatment.

5 FINAL CONSIDERATIONS

Many hospitals still lack the presence of psychologists as part of their healthcare teams. However, it is already possible to see this great contribution and the repercussions of the important role played by psychologists in the care of hospitalized patients or those undergoing invasive, painful treatments, causing psychic reactions that lead doctors to recognize the value and importance of this interdisciplinary work, when they realize that this is an issue that is beyond their control.

In order to ensure that the psychologist's work in hospitals continues to be satisfactory, more and more authors are willing to study and investigate this area, with the aim of contributing to and enriching the theoretical knowledge of this field, so that these services prove to be even more effective.

Thus, with regard to psychoanalysis, there are several authors who draw on this theory, showing that it is possible to adopt its techniques, placing free association as a fundamental technique, which has not been abandoned, but is indispensably used as a rule for the subject to express their subjectivity through speech, in the face of suffering and pain related to their illness.

In this way, this theory proves its real possibility by supporting practice, demystifying misconceptions about everyday clinical care and breaking the paradigm of the traditional consulting room.

As well as time, the setting is not an obstacle to psychological care taking place, so it has been shown that nothing can affect the effectiveness of psychological care in hospital, since what matters is the subjectivity of the subject, that is, what is not organic, but psychic, in which the body that exists is symbolic and only appears through words.

Therefore, the clinical case reported, as well as its discussion, has helped to show the importance of psychological care in the hospital setting, transcending all the impasses and limits of the hospital, especially the analytical setting, and also undoing the skepticism on the part of some professionals who, in turn, have a very different view of the subject from that of psychology. Thus, while psychology gives a voice to the subject, the healthcare team wants to silence this same subject, because they can't bear to deal with the pain of others.

This is once again the importance of the hospital psychologist, who also helps in this relationship between the healthcare team and the patient, because once the patient presents his complaints about his illness, it sounds distressing to some professionals in the healthcare team, demonstrating that they can't stand what can't be silenced with medication.

However, even in the face of all the difficulties that psychologists face in their work in the hospital environment, they must make every effort to continue to develop this very important work aimed at the patient's quality of life, reducing the suffering of the individual who is affected by an illness, whether acute or chronic, and is going through a painful and painful process in both the physical and psychological senses.

REFERENCES:

ALBERTI, SONIA. The hospital, the subject, psychoanalysis. **Rev. SBPH** v.11 n.1, Rio de Janeiro, June, 2008.

ALMEIDA, RAQUEL A. Possibilities of using brief psychotherapy in a general hospital. **Rev.SBPH** v.13 n.1, Rio de Janeiro, Jun., 2010.

BOTEGA (ORG.), NEURY J. **Reapao a Doenpa e a hospitalizapao**. In: Psychiatric Practice in the General Hospital. 3ª ed. Porto Alegre: Artmed, 2012.

BRANT, JOSEANE APARECIDA DE S. **On the tightrope of death... Or life? Children and chronic renal failure.** In: Psychoanalysis and the Hospital - Children and their pain. Rio de Janeiro: Revinter, 1999.

BRAZIL [Constitution (1988)]. **Constitution of the Federative Republic of Brazil**: promulgated on October 5, 1988. Text organization: Chamber of Deputies. 35th ed. Brasilia: Camara, 2012. Digital Library of the Chamber of Deputies.< http://bd.camara.gov.br> accessed on: 22/05/2016.

CAMON (ORG.), VALDEMAR AUGUSTO A.; ET AL.**O Psicologo no Hospital.** In: Hospital psychology: theory and practice. 1st ed. Sao Paulo: Pioneira Thomson Learning, 2003.

CAMPOS, DENISE T. F. **Care and the subject: questions about the expanded clinic.** In: Processes of subjectivation, expanded clinic and psychic suffering. 1st ed. Rio de Janeiro: Cia de Freud, 2012.

CAMPOS, TEREZINHA C.P. **Psicologia Hospitalar: a atuapao do psicologo em hospitais.** 1st ed. Sao Paulo: E.P.U.,1995

CANTARELLI, ANA PAULA S. Novas abordagens da atuapao do psicologo no contexto hospitalar. **Rev. SBPH** v. 12 n. 2, Rio de Janeiro, Dec., 2009.

CATANI, JULIA. The role of the analytical framework in the hospital context: possibilities and limits of action. **Rev. Psicologia e Saude** v. 5 n. 1 Jan./Jun. 2013.

CESARINO, CLAUDIA B.; CASAGRANDE, LISETE D.R. Patients with chronic renal failure undergoing hemodialysis treatment: activity

nurse education. **Rev. Latino-Am** v. 6 n. 4, Ribeirao Preto, Oct., 1998.

DIAS, NATALIA M.; RADOMILE, MARIA EUGENIA S. The implementation of the psychology service in the general hospital: a proposal of development of instruments and procedures for action. **Rev. SBPH** v. 09 n. 2, Rio de Janeiro, Dec., 2006.

ELIAS, VALERIA A. Psicanalise no hospital: algumas considerapoes a partir de Freud. **Rev. SBPH** v. 11 n. 1, Rio de Janeiro, Jun. 2008.

FREUD, S. (1912) **Recommendations for doctors practicing psychoanalysis.** In: Complete Works, Vol. XII. Rio de Janeiro: Imago. Ed, 2006.

(1913) **On the beginning of treatment (New recommendations on the technique of psychoanalysis).** In: Complete Works, Vol. XII. Rio de Janeiro: Imago. Ed, 2006.

(1914) **Remember, Repeat and Elaborate (New recommendations on the technique of psychoanalysis II).** In: Complete Works, Vol. XII. Rio de Janeiro: Imago. Ed, 2006.

(1914[1915]) **On Narcissism: An Introduction.** In: Complete Works, Vol. XIV. Rio de Janeiro: Imago. Ed, 2006.

(1915) **Reflections for times of war and death - II Our attitude towards death.** In: Complete Works, Vol. XIV. Rio de Janeiro: Imago. Ed, 2006.

(1917 [1915]) **Mourning and Melancholy.**In: Obras Completas, Vol.XIV. Rio de Janeiro: Imago. Ed, 2006.

(1919[1918]) **Lines of progress in psychoanalytic therapy.** In: Complete Works, Vol. XVII. Rio de Janeiro: Imago. Ed, 2006.

(1926) **The question of lay analysis.** In: Complete Works, Vol. XX. Rio de Janeiro: Imago. Ed, 2006.

GIOIA-MARTINS (ORG), DINORAH F. **Saúde e doenpa: um breve historico - como e onde o psicologo pode atuar?** In: Psychology and Health: Training, Research and Professional Practice. 1ª ed. Sao Paulo: Vetor, 2012.

ISMAEL, SILVIA MARIA C. **A Pratica Psicologica e Sua Interface com as Doengas.** 2ª ed. Sao Paulo: Casa do Psicologo, 2010

JORGE, MARCO ANTONIO C.; FERREIRA, NADIA P. **Freud, creator of psychoanalysis.** 3rd ed. Rio de Janeiro: Zahar, 2010.

JUGEND, MAIANA; JURKIEWICZ RACHEL. Psychological assistance through clinical listening during hospitalization. **Rev. SBPH** v.15 n. 1, Rio de Janeiro, Jan./Jun. 2012.

KERN, E. C.; BORNHOLDT, E. Psicologia Hospitalar: definigoes e possibilidades de insergao profissional. **Psicologia: Ciencia e Profissao** v.24 n.3, Brasilia, September, 2004.

KUBLER-ROSS, ELIZABETH. **On death and dying.** 1st ed. Sao Paulo: Martins Fontes, 1996.

LAZZARETTI, CLAIRE TEREZINHA, ET AL.Manual de Psicologia Hospitalar.21a ed. Curitiba: Unificado.**Coletanea Conexao Psi**. Technical Series SBPH - Brazilian Society of Hospital Psychology. Official website of the institution. <http://www.portal.crppr.org.br/pagina/cadernos-e- manuals> accessed on: 02/05/2016, 2007.

MORETTO, MARIA L. T. **What can an analyst do in hospital?** 1st ed. Sao Paulo: Casa do Psicologo, 2002.

MOHALLEM, LEA N. **Psychoanalysis and the Hospital: a Space for Creation.** In: Psychoanalysis and the Hospital 3 - Time and Death: From Urgency to the Analytic Act. Rio de Janeiro: Revinter, 2003.

OLIVEIRA, IRANI T. DE; ANGELUCCI, CARLA B. **Challenges for psychologist training: school services and community care**. In: Psychology and Health: Training, Research and Professional Practice. 1st ed. Sao Paulo: Vetor, 2012.

OLIVEIRA, WAEL DE. **An Unexpected Time.** In: Psicanalise e Hospital 3 - Tempo e Morte: Da urgência ao Ato Analitico. Rio de Janeiro: Revinter, 2003.

ROMANO, WILMA B. **Principios para a pratica da psicologia clinica em hospitais.** 1st ed. Sao Paulo, Casa do Psicologo, 1999.

SALTO, MARIA CRISTINA E. **O Psicologo no Contexto Hospitalar: Uma Visão psicodramática.** Psicologia Brasil, Federagao Brasileira de Psicodrama. v.5 n.39, Sao Paulo, Mar.,2007.http://www.febrap.org.br accessed on: 16/04/2016

SANTOS, CLAUDIA T. D; SEBASTIANI, R. W. **Psychological support for the chronically ill**. In: E a psicologia entrou no hospital. 3ª ed. Sao Paulo, Cencage Learning, 2013.

SEBASTIANI, RICARDO W.; ET AL. **Hospital psychology: theory and practice.** ia ed. Sao Paulo: Pioneira Thomson Learning, 2003.

SIMONETTI, A. **Manual of hospital psychology: The map of illness.** 7th ed. Sao Paulo: Casa do psicologo, 2013.

. **Hospital Psychology and Psychoanalysis.** 1st ed. Sao Paulo: Casa do psicologo, 2015.

SOARES, CLAUDIA P. **Is there a psychoanalysis of the body?** In: Psicanalise e Hospital - A crianga e sua dor. Rio de Janeiro: Revinter, 1999.

MIX
Papier aus verantwortungsvollen Quellen
Paper from responsible sources
FSC® C105338

Printed by Books on Demand GmbH, Norderstedt / Germany